Make Tim

For Creativity

Make Time For Creativity

Finding Space for Your Most Meaningful Work

Brandon Stosuy

Abrams Image,
New York

Editor: Karrie Witkin
Designer: Kristian Henson
Production Manager:
Rebecca Westall

ISBN: 978-1-4197-4653-6

Abrams Image products are
available at special discounts
when purchased in quantity
for premiums and promotions
as well as fundraising or
educational use. Special
editions can also be created
to specification. For details,
contact specialsales@
abramsbooks.com or the
address below.

Abrams Image® is a
registered trademark of
Harry N. Abrams, Inc.

ABRAMS The Art of Books
195 Broadway, New York, NY 10007
abramsbooks.com

MIX
Paper from
responsible sources
FSC™ C144853

Contents

Introduction 7

Chapter 1: Work-Life Balance 17

Chapter 2: Daily Rituals 49

Chapter 3: Intentions and Goals 83

Chapter 4: Downtime and Creativity 117

Acknowledgments 144

"My only concern about art collaborations is that I never thought of myself as an artist."

Sufjan Stevens*
(Singer-songwriter,
Carrie & Lowell,
Illinois, Michigan)

"I still feel weird about saying that I'm an artist, just because people assume that you're well-off or you're taken care of, and you don't actually have a job."

Emma Kohlmann†
(Visual artist)

* Stosuy, Brandon, "It's Sufjan Stevens' Way or the Highway," *Interview*, November 30, 2009.
† Stosuy, Brandon, "On Becoming Comfortable with the Idea of Being an Artist," Creative Independent, November 1, 2018.

"I identify myself as a sculptor, but at the passport desk I put 'artist.'"

Matthew Barney[*]
(Multimedia artist,
creator of the
Cremaster Cycle)

You may not think of yourself as an artist, and that's fine. Many people I know who could be labeled as "artists" don't see themselves as artists, either. I've spoken to writers, musicians, filmmakers, dancers, visual artists, and the like who see what they do as work, and when they create, they're simply working—they save the word "artist" for their taxes, passport forms, and polite cocktail conversations.

This is a legitimate way to view making things. The majority of people doing creative work don't make a living from it (or any money at all), so it's important to create for the sake and love of creating in and of itself. This way, even if nobody but you knows that you get up early or go to bed late to finish your project, you keep on going.

I've had a day job my whole life. While it hasn't always been easy, I've always managed to find the time to create. I've never been a full-time artist, though. Does this mean I'm not an artist? I don't think so.

* Stosuy, Brandon, "An Interview with Matthew Barney," *Believer*, January 1, 2007.

Making Time for What Matters

There are countless creative people who work part-time or behind the scenes, people you'll never see mentioned on the front pages who've contributed to films, books, art exhibitions, and theater pieces. Not everyone gets the glory or notoriety, but the work they do is still essential (and creative).

I've put on shows at dozens of venues, facilitated tours for the musicians I manage, and organized art and music events at places like MoMA PS1, the New Museum, the Hirshhorn Museum, and the Broad Museum, but I haven't always seen my name affixed to a write-up or article. That's OK. I know what I put into it and can feel proud that it made it out into the world, and that's enough for me.

In fact, a large part of my creative output is about bringing ideas and people together. I'm a collaborator, and a firm believer in the act of collaboration, and I'm not strictly a maker of things. I see this book as a collaboration with you because without your input, it's incomplete.

Let's start our project together here by having you answer a few questions about your own creative impulses in the space provided.

What does the word "artist" mean to you? What kind of image
does it conjure?

_____

_____

_____

_____

_____

Do you consider yourself an artist? If not, why? If so, what
kind of an artist?

_____

_____

_____

_____

_____

What's your passion project? I mean, what do you do outside
of your normal day job or responsibilities? (Or, what is
it you find yourself wanting to dedicate time to even if it
doesn't pay the bills, or pay anything at all?)

_____

_____

_____

_____

_____

Do you find yourself gravitating to a specific area of creativity? What do you have a knack for, or what seems to come easy to you and bring you a sense of fulfillment in the process? (It could be hosting dinner parties, planning trips, fundraising for a cause, starting businesses, etc.)

_____

_____

_____

_____

_____

_____

_____

_____

If you had to "brand" your specific, unique approach to creativity, what would it be? Write down a word or a phrase or a sentence.

_____

_____

_____

_____

_____

Write down a hypothetical answer to the question "What do you do?" that doesn't involve what you do for paid work. What did you write?

_____

_____

_____

_____

_____

_____

_____

Look at your responses to these questions. In your day-to-day life, do you make enough time for this?

Make Time for Creativity is the first volume in a three-part series meant to guide people through different aspects of a creative life. Whether or not you view yourself as an artist, this book (and the series) is for you.

The book looks at different aspects of finding time for your passion project. I divided it into four chapters: Work-Life Balance, Daily Rituals, Intentions and Goals, and Downtime and Creativity. In each section, I discuss my own experiences, while also weaving in advice, revelations, and experiences of different types of working artists, including musicians, authors, filmmakers, dancers, designers, and visual artists. For these, I approached friends and people I've collaborated with at one time or another because I wanted the book to feel like a community gathering.

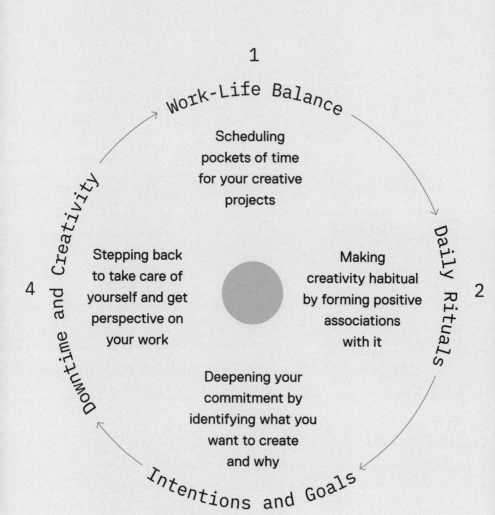

1

Work-Life Balance

Scheduling pockets of time for your creative projects

Daily Rituals

2

Making creativity habitual by forming positive associations with it

Downtime and Creativity

4

Stepping back to take care of yourself and get perspective on your work

Deepening your commitment by identifying what you want to create and why

Intentions and Goals

3

The people who ended up here are not random, and the majority of the quotations came directly from me asking for something very specific to help illuminate the creative process for you, the reader. (The handful of other quotes, like the ones at the start of this introduction, came from previous conversations I've had with creative people across a variety of platforms.)

Their quotations then led me to create different prompts about mind-set, goals, ideas, frustrations, triumphs, balance, lack of balance, and staying healthy through these ups and downs. The number of voices allowed me to build an eclectic collection of thoughts for each chapter, giving you the space to see yourself somewhere in the mix and to also see something new.

What's most important when you're reflecting on these questions, quotations, and prompts, and writing down your own answers and insights, is finding relevance and inspiration and equal footing for yourself and your own brand of creativity.

Whether you see it like this or not at this point, you're an artist, too, and what you put into this book is what completes it and is, ultimately, what makes it worthwhile.

Let's get started.

"I tend to work incrementally—adding little bits with each work session, or reviewing and adjusting work done previously. After a certain amount of time, these little bits accumulate, and then something becomes evident. Working more hours on something, pushing to speed the development, doesn't always work, in my opinion."

David Byrne
(Multimedia creator,
front person of Talking Heads)

In this chapter, I'll ask you to reflect upon your day-to-day schedule and to start looking for ways to make more time for your passion projects.

Work-life balance isn't just about balancing hours spent at work versus doing your own thing. It's also about maintaining an identity that isn't completely defined by your work (paid or unpaid) and your other responsibilities.

In this case, the "life" part of the work-life equation is your creative life, which is distinct from your downtime (we'll talk more about that in chapter 4).

A large part of feeling satisfied in your creative projects relates to sense of self. It's easier to feel positive and good when you figure out how to put more time toward your creative, personal, non-work time.

I've asked a number of working artists about how they manage their time. I've learned from them, and from my own experience, that working incrementally is ultimately beneficial to the creative process (even when time is frustratingly limited).

Here, we'll look at strategies for locating inner balance (knowing that life is a seesaw and balance is never fixed) and test out some practical time management tasks.

Finding Balance

It's hard to find the right balance, whether it's the balance between your job and creative work, or any type of work and rest. There are only so many hours in a day.

Since I was thirteen, I've always had a job. I've worked on farms, in construction, in multiple convenience stores and gas stations, at bookstores and greenhouses, and at a B-level movie theater. I was once paid to help a man write a book about how Jesus faked his death, which led to me helping the author's friend write a screenplay starring himself as a handsome international spy, all while also curating, organizing, and writing.

I've been in the creative industry for the past fifteen years, and yet I continue to work on my own side projects. One thing I've learned is that even if your job is in a creative field, your daily work might not be all that creative. Or this: if you love your job, you have the added challenge of being heavily invested in your work and finding time for your passion projects. It's hard to compartmentalize something that takes up a good deal of your day and headspace.

Dissatisfaction with your nine-to-five can lead to strong outside creative work. When you escape, you end up with a greater creative urgency. Sometimes stress leads to productivity, but using stress can catch up with you. It's not a sustainable motivator.

I've had physical jobs and sit-around jobs, social jobs and solitary jobs, tedious jobs and creative jobs; each one has offered up its own benefits and challenges, and each time I've had to figure out different techniques for maintaining my own creative momentum. For me, the key is to identify creative tasks that can be done in pockets of downtime throughout the workday and workweek, rather than waiting for a day of uninterrupted free time.

You may wonder why someone who makes art full-time could offer a useful perspective to someone who doesn't make art full-time.

Artists stand in a unique place on the subject of work-life balance. A few get paid for their art; their art is their work. Others hold paid jobs that are separate from their art. Many fall in a gray area and make both commercial and unpaid art.

No matter their situation, though, all artists have decided that making art is a critical part of their identity. Paid or unpaid, it is a high priority.

What we can learn from artists is seeing how they prioritize their creativity—both in terms of the time spent on it and how they use it to define themselves.

Your Work Vs. Creative Work

Think about how much of your identity is tied to your work and your creativity. Use these circles to map your talents and interests into two categories: "Work" and "Creative Work." Aspects that fall into both categories should go in the area where the circles overlap. Ask yourself the questions below:

1. In the "Work" circle, jot down all of your talents and interests that are accessed by your job (which could mean your career, paid work, unpaid responsibilities, or school). What comes easily to you? What do you enjoy the most? What do you find challenging in a rewarding way?

2. In the "Creative Work" circle, jot down any talents and interests that you channel into your personal projects but that don't play a role in your work. What creative challenges do you enjoy? Are you developing a latent talent or trying something new?

3. This part takes some introspection: In the middle area, jot down the talents, interests, and aspects of your personality that serve you well at your job and in your personal creativity.

This visualization will help you answer the questions on page 25.

"When I started teaching, I had to cut down on the things I do with music, but it opened up so much space for me in terms of boundaries and building my artist self to be what I want, instead of what other people want. That, and the time I spend with students and the coursework, is actually building the underlying intentions for my own work."

JD Samson
(Musician and NYU professor,
member of Le Tigre,
cofounder of MEN and Crickets)

Symbiotic or Separate?

How would you describe the relationship between your paid work and your creative work? Are they distinct compartments? Overlapping? Complementary or symbiotic practices? Do both contribute to your sense of emotional balance, or do you feel torn in too many directions?

_____

_____

_____

_____

_____

_____

_____

_____

_____

_____

_____

_____

_____

_____

_____

_____

_____

_____

Use What Is Available

At various points in his life, the author Raymond Carver worked as a delivery person, sawmill laborer, library assistant, and janitor. When I was a teenager I read about how he did his janitorial work in the first hours of his shift, then spent the rest of the time writing. He was my favorite writer, and it felt important to me that he had to work to make a living, too. Carver's approach, born out of necessity, inspired me at the jobs I had as a teenager, and those I've had since. It taught me to think positively in situations that might not, at first glance, feel positive.

In my early twenties, I worked the graveyard shift at a Shell gas station in Western Canada. It wasn't the most traveled of places, so there were hours each night when nobody came in—it's how I ended up reading more than I'd managed to read in a typical college literature class. When people did come in and saw a kid behind the counter trying to make his way through James Joyce's *Ulysses*, it sparked interesting conversations.

When I worked the delivery job, there was downtime between calls, and I'd use those moments to scribble ideas into a spiral notebook. Construction was harder, because it demanded a certain level of attention; I had to keep my creative thinking to lunch breaks. I've had a few jobs like that where there's no real downtime built into the work duties, and so my only time to jot down ideas was during an official break.

As managing editor at the music website Pitchfork, I'd often skip my lunch break to give myself time to think about my outside projects: I'd bring something I could easily eat at my desk and chip away at non-work work. It's always been easy enough for me to coordinate and curate events at work because inboxes don't discriminate between different kinds of work.

My friend Thomas Hooper, who's a tattoo artist and a fine artist, told me that many of his ideas come to him during the day, while he's tattooing a client. He clicks into his task of guiding the needle through the person's skin, and possibilities for other projects come to mind. There's something about the structure and constraints of a job that encourages us to daydream. Take note of what comes up.

Think about a normal day in your own life. What are the best ways to integrate your creative work into your daily life? Are there parts of the paid workday you could reclaim?

"I need about five minutes to reread a poem I love a couple of times, depending on the poem. That's all."

Hanif Abdurraqib
(Poet/writer, author of
They Can't Kill Us Until They Kill Us,
A Fortune for Your Disaster, and
Go Ahead in the Rain)

Micro Productivity

Try this exercise: Break a passion project into different-sized increments. First, list the things that you can do in the smallest packet of time to meaningfully contribute to your art practice:

In five minutes, I can . .

_____

_____

_____

_____

In ten minutes, I can . . .

_____

_____

_____

_____

_____

In fifteen minutes, I can . . .

_____

_____

_____

_____

_____

Yes, things like sharpening your pencils, doing calf stretches, or ordering guitar strings all count.

Maximum Productivity

What is the largest packet of time that you can productively spend on your art? Be honest with yourself about the way you work. Think about how much time you need to settle into your task, how long your attention span lasts, and whether you feel any physical strain after working for a while. I find that after two hours, I start checking email and lose focus on writing. So, for me, setting aside an entire day to write doesn't get the greatest results for the time spent. Here are a few other perspectives:

"I have a fifteen-minute hourglass my wife gave me last year. Three turns on the hourglass and I've often gotten somewhere in my work. Perhaps this forty-five-minute period correlates with other units, like dream cycles or the typical therapy session."

Prem Krishnamurthy
(Graphic designer, curator, founder of IN-FO.CO and Wkshps)

"I need a minimum of six hours to get actual writing done. Smaller amounts of time I can use for correspondence and business-y stuff, but making work requires vast swaths of uninterrupted time. My 'writing process' is extremely indirect and distracted and doesn't look like much to the outside observer; it's mostly about trying to get in touch with the parts of my brain that have managed to evade society's prescribed orderliness, where the mind is free to wander."

Elaine Kahn

(Poet, author of *Women in Public* and *I Told You I Was Sick: A Romance*)

Your Sweet Spot

Do you find yourself empathizing with either of these approaches: Elaine's need for long periods of uninterrupted time or Prem's forty-five-minute stints?

_____

_____

_____

_____

_____

_____

_____

_____

_____

_____

_____

_____

_____

_____

_____

_____

_____

Try the Opposite

If you need several consecutive hours to get any creative work done, set a timer for forty-five minutes to see what you accomplish. On the flip side, if you typically get distracted after about an hour, see whether you can extend your productivity by taking a series of fifteen-minute breaks. Record any observations here.

"I find that integrating as much creativity into my routine helps me for when I am working on larger projects. I sing and dance every morning. I keep a detailed dream journal, which I draw from a lot in my projects. I like to listen to specific music while I work on projects, and keep in mind how that music will influence what I'm making. I like to layer bird sounds over music while editing poetry. I do a lot of journaling in the morning, but usually nighttime is when I pull things together or come up with my ideas for projects."

Chariot Wish
(Poet, visual artist,
co-editor of Glo Worm Press)

The Creative To-Do List

Write your own creative to-do list. Ignore the practical for a second and make a list of what you would do if you could structure your time entirely around your creativity.

—   —

—   —

—   —

—   —

—   —

—   —

—   —

—   —

—   —

—   —

The Done List

Today, keep this page marked and list everything that you do. Include the mundane, seemingly insignificant, and non-creative stuff, along with anything that you were able to do toward your creative practice. Date the bottom of the page. Do you feel a sense of accomplishment?

—   —

—   —

—   —

—   —

—   —

—   —

—   —

—   —

—   —

"Making realistic lists of what I need to finish each day and week helps me feel focused and encouraged. On days where I feel like I've 'gotten nothing done,' having a record of ten small projects I knocked out gives me perspective and a sense of accomplishment."

Sadie Dupuis
(Musician, poet, solo artist, and front person of Speedy Ortiz)

Morning

"I get up at 5:00 a.m. and have one hour entirely dedicated to my inner self. I make myself a coffee, stretch for a few minutes, then sit down on my couch and check in with my body. I just sit and see where my thoughts go. After that I meditate. I call it 'dropping into my heart.' This routine has been a game changer for me. I used to get up and jump on my computer. I don't do that anymore and actually feel more productive this way."

Tina Roth Eisenberg
(Founder of *swissmiss*, Tattly, and CreativeMornings)

How you start your day sets the tone for that day. What if you resisted the urge to pick up your phone and plug into the outside world first thing in the morning? What if you started by taking just ten minutes of quiet time for yourself?

Award-winning designer Prem Krishnamurthy has honed a morning discipline of jumping right into his creative work, while avoiding obstacles like the news and outside interaction: "Writing or designing something new requires as clear of a mindspace as I can muster. This often means waking up early and writing fast and furious in a document before I do anything else—especially checking email, phones, or other devices."

If being creative is a priority for you, find a way to nudge that side of yourself awake first, before anything else can influence your processing.

Starting Up

Set yourself up for success by spending fifteen minutes each
morning doing something that inspires you, perhaps while
having your coffee.

MONDAY	TUESDAY	WEDNESDAY
THURSDAY	FRIDAY	SATURDAY
SUNDAY		

Read a poem, flip through an art book, or listen to a
piece of music. Jot down an idea for each day and
set up your music, books, journal, or anything else
that you need the night before; don't leave it up to
your groggy morning brain!

Work-Life Balance

Reflections

Jot down any observations (what worked, what didn't) after a
week of these kinds of mornings. Can you refine the practice?
If your mornings are too demanding, is there another part of
the day that you can reclaim (maybe your lunch break)?

_____

_____

_____

_____

_____

_____

_____

_____

_____

_____

_____

_____

_____

_____

_____

_____

Routine and Consistency

> "My writing rituals are always changing, but they always involve some sort of constraint, even if it's as simple as a time constraint. For some reason, when I write down in my calendar, 'write from 9 a.m. to 1 p.m.,' I will actually do it, because it feels like I have to."

Chelsea Hodson

(Writer, teacher, and author of
Tonight I'm Someone Else)

For all of the analysis and suggestions, a successful creative process often boils down to something that sounds simple on paper but is difficult, at first, to achieve in reality: You need the discipline to do what you say you're going to do when you say you're going to do it, even if nobody's watching you and you're only saying it to yourself. This means putting time and effort into your project, even if nobody's telling you to do it, or keeping tabs on whether or not you do it. It can be a hard thing to do.

I've spoken to people about how they stay productive. Many people focus on repetition: They find a schedule or a routine that works and stick to it. You do what you need to find consistency. A sustainable practice isn't one that involves working furiously for a day, then doing nothing for a month. With an inconsistent rhythm, you won't see results. Spending fifteen minutes a day on your creative project will 100 percent be more useful than doing nothing for a month, then spending an entire day trying to catch up, and then going fallow again for weeks.

It's helpful to feel calm when you work. When you're operating from a place of panic or guilt, this sort of zone is harder to locate. The time you set aside doesn't need to be hours and hours, and none of that time needs to be taken up with you feeling bad about yourself. Accept that some sessions will be more productive than others. Musician Stephen O'Malley recently told me, "I just finished a project that took ten years. I recently made a piece of music in an hour."

The time you have available is never a judgment on the work you're doing. If the block you can devote is the time it takes to drive to your office, then use that time; if you commit to it over and over, you'll make progress, and after a few months, be shocked at how much you've managed to create.

Social Media

I know people who tell me they don't have the time to work on a creative project, then spend hours a day on social media. One day I realized Facebook notifications made me feel like I couldn't focus on anything, and the act of "liking" felt useless (like clicking through channels on a television), so I decided to deactivate it, and I removed Instagram and Twitter from my phone. These simple actions helped me make downtime more productive.

What's your relationship to social media? Which platforms are most useful to you? Are there any platforms you could quit? If you're able to let even just one platform go, you'll have more time in your day to create.

Social media can also be useful in getting your creative work out into the world, so maybe you'll find it more useful to just deactivate an account for a bit, or parts of the day, while you're in the middle of making something. Start small.

What if you left your phone at your workstation and took a notebook with you to lunch? Try this one day and see what happens.

"The big thing I realized is that instead of just saying I need to find a balance, I became more proactive on setting myself up for that balance: requesting time off when I need it, knowing when to step away from too many social engagements, making sure my house is clean and the fridge stocked."

Shanekia Mcintosh
(Poet, performer, artist, librarian)

Conclusion

This section was about balancing your sense of self by figuring out how to put more time toward your creative side, your passion project, and your personal, non-work self. Your paying job and other responsibilities are just one part of your identity, but because most of us need to spend quite a bit of time at work, it tends to overshadow other areas of our lives.

Having a project that's self-determined and maybe just for fun is one way of balancing your time and, in the process, your sense of self. You are more than your paid work, and your non-work time should be treated meaningfully.

Finding time for your creative pursuits means examining the way you habitually spend time and changing those habits. Start by deliberately scheduling sessions for your project. Don't dismiss the small increments of time that are available to you. Reframe anything in your daily life that inspires you or develops your skills as a creative act, and give yourself credit for being available to it.

Before you turn the page, open your calendar for the next
month and find the open spots for some aspect of your creative
practice. Schedule them like you would a meeting and set up
reminders. Write them down in your planner, if you use one.
Start with these challenges:

> Look at your Micro Productivity list
on page 29 and try scheduling two or
three fifteen-minute sessions each week,
knowing exactly how you will use them.

> Then look for at least one larger
block of time (the ideal amount that you
feel will be productive—see page 32) and
schedule it.

> Review your Creative To-Do List on
page 35. Can you schedule a retreat for
yourself; a day that resembles this one
as much as possible?

"Ritualizing life and domestic tasks, as well as spaces and creative processes, helps add diligence and dedication to my practice as an artist, and it also heightens the meaning of my life and my work, makes everything feel a bit more magical and sacred."

Shanekia Mcintosh
(Poet, performer, artist, librarian)

In the previous chapter, I asked you to evaluate your day-to-day and to find ways to make time for your passion projects. This chapter is about coming up with specific rituals that will support the good habits you want to create.

You'll read about the rituals of different people—musicians, writers, dancers, filmmakers, designers, poets. It can be inspiring to see how other people get their work done, and maybe you'll see a bit of yourself in them and their approaches.

There are also prompts to help you start thinking more carefully about your rituals. We'll explore how rituals help you transition from your daily roles to your creative work, and we'll focus on how rituals make you feel present for your creative practice and able to treat it like sacred time.

I use the word "mind-set" a lot because it's especially important in creative work. I find it most productive to come from a positive space. Rituals help me get there.

So, get into whatever space or mind-set that works best for you, and let's get going.

Establishing a routine for your creative work is essential, but it's only half the battle. We all know routines can be, or get, boring—and if something is boring, it can fall by the wayside over time.

Adding ritual aspects to a creative project makes it seem important and worth pursuing. Making something feel pleasurable and not like a chore can help to make it stick. Once that ritual becomes part of your everyday, you look forward to it. It feels satisfying. It completes your day. You feel weird if you don't do it.

Rituals also help slow things down, something we all need help with in the digital age. Just about everybody deals with feeling too busy or overwhelmed, and it can be difficult to remove ourselves from that scattered mind-set of constant phone checking and browser refreshing.

Rituals help do that by elevating the everyday and offering an opportunity to look at yourself and your projects more closely. They can snap us out of rote routine into a more thoughtful and mindful place. Rituals can make you available to certain aspects of yourself—your physical self, your spiritual self—that might not otherwise get attention over the course of the day.

All of that said, even if you are pragmatic and understated about what you do—and even if you are not particularly spiritual—you may still find it motivating to reframe an aspect of your routine as a ritual. Not all rituals require an altar.

My writing ritual is not that colorful: When I wake up to write, I sit on the same side of the couch, with the same mug on the same shelf. That may seem very basic and unimportant, but it helps me establish a specific mood, one that makes me feel calm and comfortable and ready to work. It's become a ritual. A sacred place. It also elevates the everyday, making the act of writing feel special.

While I can explain the value of ritual and offer examples of mine and of other people I know, there's no universal way. Everyone's process is unique. But if you're drawing a blank, sometimes hearing how other people do it can help you think of ways to do it yourself.

How do you transform a routine into a ritual?

Ritual = Habit + Magic

> "I think of ritual as a process of making something important by meditating or initiating something into the divine, or using habit, repetition, and objects to engage with the divine."

Chariot Wish
(Poet, visual artist, co-editor
of Glo Worm Press)

Creating a ritual begins by making positive associations. Think of something you enjoy and pair it with the work. It's a bit Pavlovian. Like the way the smell of cut grass can remind you of a long-ago summer, a ritual becomes a positive association with your hard and often unpaid creative work.

Choose a particular space, a kind of lighting, a scent, a taste, a sound, or a type of music. Make sure where you do the work is comfortable. In some sense, it's like you're allowing your life to become art. Your living room, your kitchen, your yard, the space around your desk (or your makeshift desk) all have potential to become an extension of your creative project. You are curating a moment—or a space—that you want to enter each day.

Seem like too much? I don't think so. You should see what you're doing as important and worthy of this kind of treatment. What you're doing is important and worthy of this treatment.

Reflections

Jot down as much as you can about how you currently go about preparing yourself for your creative work. It's useful to think in terms of the basic five senses: sight, smell, sound, taste, touch. Can you include details for each?

Associations Matrix

Think about the associations you've developed. A positive association might be a song from your childhood; hearing just a fragment of it transports you back to a specific time, place, feeling, and maybe even what the weather was like. On the flip side, you may associate a specific scent with a difficult boss, and you shut down a little whenever you smell it.

1. Use this chart to loosely organize the random associations (positive and negative) that you have with your work (job) and your creative work (or favorite pastime).

2. Look for patterns in your chart. Maybe you have positive associations with your job (such as "comfortable chair" or "morning chat with colleagues") that are missing from your creative work. What can you do to change that? What do you want to lean into? What do you want to move away from?

This is just another way of noticing what resonates with you on an emotional and physical level. These are the potential ingredients for your ritual.

If you don't have a consistent creative practice (or are otherwise stumped), focus on one time that you felt especially productive and "in the zone" and jot down the specifics.

WORK

POSITIVE ASSOCIATIONS

NEGATIVE ASSOCIATIONS

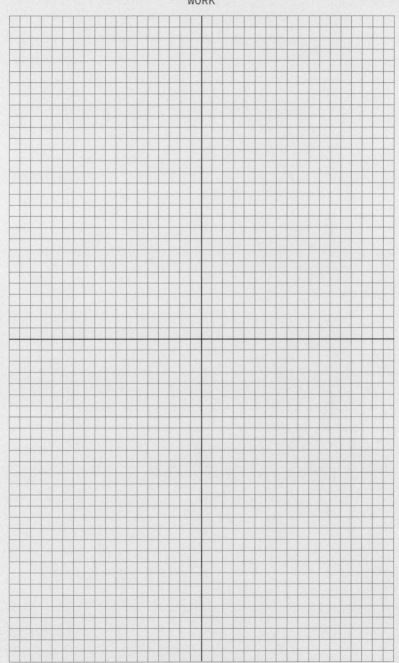

CREATIVE WORK

"I can really get into oils, teas, creams, or the smells in old theaters or even dusty, cigarette-stained rehearsal rooms. There are scents and traces of work everywhere. A ritual space leaves its traces. Those traces are energy. I feel connected to this energy when I'm working early in the morning or late at night."

Jenny Hval
(Singer-songwriter, producer,
author of *Paradise Rot*)

Pavlov's List

Keep a running list of some of your favorite things and
positive associations. Think about incorporating some of
these things into your daily practice.

—   —

—   —

—   —

—   —

—   —

—   —

—   —

—   —

—   —

—   —

Ritual and Daily Life

We've defined ritual as any practice that elevates a space or moment in the day and puts you in the best mind-set for your creative pursuits. The ritual itself is a creative act. You might use rituals throughout the day as a way of weaving a creative thread through everything else that you are doing. Or another approach: You can use ritual to remove yourself from your everyday responsibilities, to set a boundary around your creative time.

Consider these examples:

"I am one to absolutely ritualize not only my domestic life, but my artistic practice as well, and often those are one in the same to me—or through ritual and routine they become one and the same. To keep a consistent work ethic/habit in art making, I try to merge it as much as I can with my domestic life. The past few years, most of my projects have been focused around my home. In the sense that I am creating sculptures for my house and curating my space as if I was given a movie set to design. I love to curate my space as a ritual for creating, and creating is also a part of that."

Chariot Wish
(Poet, visual artist, co-editor of Glo Worm Press)

"While working on our first film, we realized how important momentum is to the creative process—as well as how both fragile and fleeting it can be. This is especially true of long-term projects for which the rewards of your hard work might not come for years (if at all). To combat the creative fatigue and imbue a sense of levity into our workflow, we began imagining our project as a military effort, complete with physical fitness requirements, code-named operations, and a war room (formerly known as 'our living room'). This somewhat silly, tongue-in-cheek reframing proved to be incredibly effective in that it provided structure and focus that allowed us the freedom to be creative and experiment in the direction of a defined goal. But beyond that, the absurdity of the whole ritual created a kind of surreal space just outside of reality in which we were able to create and innovate."

Sasha Hecht and Amelia Trask
(Cofounders of No Plus One Productions, filmmakers of *I'll Be Gone*)

Escape or Integrate?

Reread the passages representing two very different
approaches to using ritual in daily life on the previous
page. Which do you relate to the most, and why?

_____

_____

_____

_____

_____

_____

Consider reframing various parts of your daily routine as
rituals. You could do this by attaching something pleasurable
(or some small aspect of your creative work) to your
quotidian tasks. Jot down some ideas here:

_____

_____

_____

_____

_____

_____

_____

_____

How can you enhance the time and space that you carve out of your daily life for your creative projects? Try giving this time its own name and identity. What will you call it? Write a mission statement or perhaps jot down three rules that apply to your creative space.

_____

_____

_____

_____

_____

_____

_____

_____

_____

_____

_____

_____

_____

_____

_____

_____

_____

_____

Ritual Spaces

You never create work in a vacuum: the space where you're working is important to your process. Some people are homebodies, while others need to get out of their homes to create. Some people put a lot of thought and knickknacks into their environment, while others are quite minimal (but still specific) in their needs.

I once lived in a friend's closet in Portland, Oregon. My desk was made out of milk cartons. On the surface this may sound terrible, but I found the confined space useful for focusing. Having so few belongings made it easier to work than to procrastinate. I would wake up and write in silence until I heard my hosts moving around before I would emerge. It was not a sustainable arrangement, but it really worked for me at the time.

Consider the following approaches to ritual space. Note how they integrate play and experimentation.

"My bedroom is where I do most of my work, and I'm specific about having colored lights, pink and red and purple—those, I have found, are my favorite! And I am specific about my bedsheets; I don't have a desk yet, so I just work in my bed."

Chariot Wish
(Poet, visual artist, co-editor of Glo Worm Press)

"My preference is to get up before seven and get out of the house quite quickly. I like to go to a café to write, drink black coffee, and just start typing or writing by hand for a couple of hours. Then I can do other things, or keep writing in a different place. But I enjoy the ritual of starting in a public place. All I need is good coffee and mediocre music playing. I am very good at blocking out sound. Perhaps it's something I need to do to go deep inside myself?"

Jenny Hval
(Singer-songwriter,
producer, author of *Paradise Rot*)

Sacred Place

Describe your workspace; what works about it and what doesn't? What adjustments can you make so that it is an inviting place to create?

_____

_____

_____

_____

_____

_____

_____

_____

_____

_____

_____

_____

_____

_____

_____

_____

Now describe your dream space for your creative pursuits. Really run with this exercise. Is it a wooden shed in the wilderness? A glass atrium on top of a skyscraper? On an ornate, cozy houseboat in Amsterdam?

"I've written to a specific soundtrack over and over again, so that writing becomes almost Pavlovian. If I hear that soundtrack, I know it's writing time."

Chelsea Hodson
(Writer, teacher, author of
Tonight I'm Someone Else)

When I run, I listen to the same albums: *The Earth Is Not a Cold Dead Place* by Explosions in the Sky and *Ordinary Corrupt Human Love* by Deafheaven. The music is expansive and anthemic, with spacious guitars and big dynamics. Explosions in the Sky does not have a vocalist. Deafheaven does, but his words are indecipherable, and his howls blend with the other sounds. These records create a soundtrack to my morning miles, and I'll often find myself close to tears. It's a therapeutic outpouring; one that, on a practical level, allows me to gauge where I am in the workout because I've gotten so used to matching the miles to a particular song.

Sometimes when I sit down to write I'll put on my headphones and never press Play. I work in silence, but having the headphones in place removes me from the room around me and allows me to focus. There are rituals that calm you down, while others get you pumped up. I find it's good to have both options, and that it's easiest for me to find the right mood for the moment with sound.

Playlist

What music do you find inspiring?

_____

_____

_____

_____

What music relaxes you?

_____

_____

_____

_____

What music psychs you up?

_____

_____

_____

_____

Does some music do all of the above?

_____

_____

_____

_____

Experiment with sound: What happens if you listen to louder, quieter, faster, or slower music? Have you tried working in silence? What about listening to people talking (audiobooks or podcasts), or nature sounds?

"I always do a two-minute 'star pose' before taking the stage. I spread my legs and arms and take up as much space as I can, and after about a minute and a half, something about the blood flow gives me a shot of adrenaline."

Haley Fohr
(Vocalist, composer, producer, Circuit des Yeux)

"I have an app called 7 Minute Vocal Warm Up, and there's a breathing warm-up on there. I've been doing that pretty much every time I have to do something challenging to my psyche. I teach so often about being aware of your body and breath and how that plays into your 'performance' of life or art. I have been more tuned into doing that myself."

JD Samson
(Musician and NYU professor, member of Le Tigre, cofounder of MEN and Crickets)

"I want to work without anger, so I have found a way to get rid of it first thing in the morning. On weekdays, I wake up early and wear myself out by doing a variety of very strenuous activities. This gets rid of the anger and helps me make better decisions."

Matthew Day Jackson
(Visual artist)

"I like to clean my kitchen—like really get in there. It helps me clear my thoughts and get to work, especially when I'm feeling anxious with the writing process. If I get inspired, or something just comes to me, I stop everything and write it down."

Shanekia Mcintosh
(Poet, performer, artist, librarian)

"I exorcise the resistance first. I scream, sing, swing my body, or meditate, I spread all my notes all over the table, or I put on a song and allow myself an improvisational five-minute dance and then I put my fingers to the computer or pen to the paper and begin. Following my intuition for whatever I physically crave first for a few minutes, and then I settle into my projects."

Sigrid Lauren
(Dancer, choreographer, performance artist, member of FlucT)

Use Your Body

Sometimes just sitting down at your workspace and expecting the magic to happen is unrealistic; as Sigrid Lauren aptly states on page 73, you need to "exorcise the resistance." Think about how the physical rituals described on the previous pages tie into each person's creative vocation. Do you ever feel anxious or restless before settling into a creative activity? Does your discipline have an impact on your body?

_____

_____

_____

_____

_____

_____

_____

_____

_____

_____

_____

_____

_____

_____

_____

_____

What kind of physical activity can you connect to your creative pursuits? Do you find breathwork useful? The act of cleaning? Maybe light stretching or something more intense, like a jog in the park? Jot down what works (or what might help) here.

_____

_____

_____

_____

_____

_____

_____

_____

_____

_____

_____

_____

_____

_____

_____

_____

_____

When people first start working out, they often follow a written routine that includes the number of sets and repetitions of each particular exercise. If it makes sense, write out your physical ritual like you would an exercise regimen. See how long it takes before it becomes second nature.

"I'm very pro-rituals, and do lots of rituals that seem to prep me for uncovering language, which include looking at and arranging my various collections of objects. I feel very connected to the creative process when I am arranging objects in particular 'scenes,' as this does seem to allow me to reconfigure language in my brain."

Dorothea Lasky
(Poet, teacher, author of *Milk* and *ROME*)

If you have an affinity for crystals, stones, and charms, you're likely already using them to access a type of energy—perhaps confidence or calmness—that is conducive to your creative practice. But you can elevate your craft and process with objects even if you aren't spiritually inclined.

Most of us have items that we feel a connection to: a family heirloom, a particular coffee mug, a sweater you've worn for years that fits just right. These objects hold meaning, memories, or positive associations that we want to keep tangible. What if you brought something like this into your creative space?

Or going a step more practical, do you use any special supplies or tools in your trade? Arranging these items in a particular way on your desk counts as a ritual. Finding the perfect pen or knife or brush is a distinct pleasure in itself and a motivation to keep making things.

Experiment with attaching meaning to objects and seeing how they support you. Musician Haley Fohr, who performs as Circuit des Yeux, describes how objects have helped her manage the emotional aspects of touring:

"I have an altar in which I charge special little charms and carry them around with me to special events—birthdays, concerts, collaborative rehearsals. Often, I choose one stone and have it next to my pedal board during shows and in my pocket during international travel. When I first began carrying a stone, it was a specific piece of obsidian that was gifted to me during a hard time. Initially I carried the stone around with me in hopes of charging myself with positive activity and allowing the obsidian to retain the darkness in my life. But slowly over the last five years, the purpose of the stone has transformed. I no longer carry obsidian, and instead have a rotation of small rocks that were gifted to me by friends and companions over the years. They reside in my workroom, where I create most days, and travel with me when I am touring. The stone is now a literal and figurative piece of my foundation, and a comfort item that I often turn to during lonely, weary travel."

Haley Fohr
(Vocalist, composer, producer, Circuit des Yeux)

Tools and Talismans

Do you relate to the concept of using ritual objects to
support your creative practice? If so, how?

_____

_____

_____

_____

_____

_____

_____

_____

_____

_____

_____

_____

_____

_____

_____

_____

Don't relate? Try this exercise: Throughout the course of a week, make note of whether the objects that you are using hold positive associations for you. Does having certain objects in particular places help you focus? Often, an object ritual is closer than you realize.

Changing Your Ritual

"I really love to do the same thing every day, until I get sick of it and need a break. I think about this a lot. I think I was born for repetition, and I really get elevated and clear-minded by repeating the same actions."

Jenny Hval

(Singer-songwriter, producer, author of *Paradise Rot*)

What's important is identifying a situation or space or scenario that brings results, and then locking that in—until it no longer works. A few of the people I spoke to about rituals mentioned this, mostly in passing: Routines and rituals can change and shift over time. You need to be open to that, and once something stops working, think about what else might instead be necessary. Don't try to keep forcing something if it's no longer helpful. It's essential you remain inspired. You want your rituals to remain special.

You need to pay attention to what works for you. You're thinking about what you find comforting, or what can put you in a positive mental space, to make work and to succeed. You need to find a way to make it enjoyable or interesting or exciting enough to keep making time for it. It's important to harness the energy, excitement, and momentum of the passion project without burning out or losing interest.

Once you think you have an idea of your rituals, try switching them up. If you find yourself working often in the morning, what happens if you try working at night? If it is effective, maybe you can find a second ritual. If it doesn't work, why do you think it didn't?

Conclusion

You might have made it this far and still be thinking: I have no rituals. This is probably not true. Sometimes you have rituals without realizing it: I noticed recently that when I write I need my space to be clutter-free. If I have that, and the coffee I've mentioned, I'm good. I'd focused so much on one aspect of my ritual and I hadn't noticed the other.

If you need some help, as we all do, and can't quite get to your creative work as often as you'd like, maybe you light a candle, burn sage, dim the lights, brew a specific kind of green tea. Or, like me, maybe your ritual is sitting in the same spot on the same couch over and over until it feels like it's your own sacred space. Try to find your own version of that place by forming positive associations with your routines and habits. Keep asking yourself:

> Do you need a specific atmosphere and space when you create? Do you need the room to feel or smell a certain way? What about sound?

> Are you best when you settle into one place, or do you need to change the environment for different tasks?

> Are you surrounded by the tools you need (practically and emotionally speaking), and does arranging these objects help you set the stage for creativity?

"When I start to work on a project I get a crystal-clear vision of precisely what the final product will look like. I chase it down. Then, the more realized the idea becomes, the more I realize I had no idea what it would actually be like. Each time this happens I'm freshly shocked to discover that I had just been hoodwinking myself all along to trick an idea out of my head. I punch my head, appalled by the shameless betrayal of my own trust. Then I sit down to work with whatever is now, thank god, in front of me. Repeat."

Vernon Chatman
(Comedy writer,
South Park writer, actor, producer)

In chapter 1, we tackled the task of finding time for creativity. In chapter 2, I asked you to come up with specific rituals to support your creative practice and make it habitual. This chapter is about staying motivated by setting goals and intentions for your work.

A goal is something you hope to achieve. It's external to yourself; a kind of mark in the future that you hope to meet. Think of it as the destination.

An intention is why you are doing the thing in the first place. An intention is about the present, and how you're feeling when you do what it is you do. In that way, it's more internal. Think about intention as how you'd feel about your work, even if nobody else ever saw it or experienced it.

As Vernon Chatman suggests, even if you think you have a clear goal in mind, you're likely to find another direction entirely in the process. But you can still meet your intentions without achieving your goals. This is an important factor in deciding if your goals are still the right ones.

In this section, we'll look at how different artists approach intention and goal setting, and we'll find ways to stay focused on the process when need be, and how to create reachable goals when that is what's needed.

Inner Drive

When I first started writing as a teenager in a dusty farming town in the woods, I had no concrete goals in mind—I enjoyed writing and expressing myself, and so I kept doing it. It temporarily transported me into a different world, and it made me happy.

My solitary writing led me to cut and paste my words together to create a zine I called *White Bread* (the title inspired, in part, by stocking loaves of bread at the convenience store where I worked). I then took the next step and distributed the zine to people outside of my hometown. At first it was to a few people, then it was to thousands. There was no plan there, either—it made me happy, it put me in touch with kids kind of like me, and I was excited to see where it went.

I usually still make work this way, with this reasoning: I like creating things, figuring out ways to organize ideas, and making the projects moving around in my head into something concrete. Finding ways to make the idea into something real, no matter what it might be, has always been the most important thing to me.

That, and reaching people. I grew up in the punk scene, and community has always been important to me. The punk ethos taught me that I liked being on the same level as the people experiencing my work. I've never been interested in hierarchies like "fan" vs. "artist." That has never been a goal of mine.

I thought of community, and how important it was to me in the first place, before I realized I could make money from any of my projects. Now my creative output consists of writing, editing, curating, managing artists, and organizing festivals, and

I'm still driven by building community. Money has never been the main goal. I want to survive, of course, but I have always worked more from a deep intention to help audiences and artists find each other and blur the lines between them.

What happened in the past is a building block to now. It's worth considering all the creative acts that brought you to your current project, too. I attribute growing up in a small town with DIY roots to a lot of what I do. It taught me to start things myself and not to wait for someone else to make things happen. The projects that I choose now, decades later, feel like part of the same continuum.

The work is important in and of itself.

"If I don't write,
I feel dead inside."

R. O. Kwon
(Writer, author of
The Incendiaries)

"Once an astrologer told me that I
have a very active nervous system and
would need to exert a lot of energy to
alleviate the spaciousness of my mind. I
was obviously stunned she spoke to this
without knowing any details about the
relevance of this to my life."

Sigrid Lauren
(Dancer, choreographer, performance
artist, member of FlucT)

"A lot of what happens in the world doesn't make sense on either a logical or narrative level, and making art helps me investigate and reflect this because art is flexible enough to accommodate the fundamental psychosis of the everyday. In this way, I think I write mainly in an attempt to understand."

Elaine Kahn

(Poet, musician, artist, author of *Women in Public* and *I Told You I Was Sick: A Romance*)

"Creativity has been my constant and stabilizing force in my life, and I feel really grateful for that. I think at times it is the thing that centers me."

Emma Kohlmann

(Visual artist)

"I am driven to create because for every curiosity I massage out of my messy and over-populated brain, there then gets to be room for something else. I love research . . . it means I am still eager for the things I don't know. And so, by the act of creation, I'm getting constant reminders that I don't know things. That I'm not the first to attempt what I am attempting. That I am small, but still climbing."

Hanif Abdurraqib

(Poet/writer, author of *They Can't Kill Us Until They Kill Us*, *A Fortune for Your Disaster*, and *Go Ahead in the Rain*)

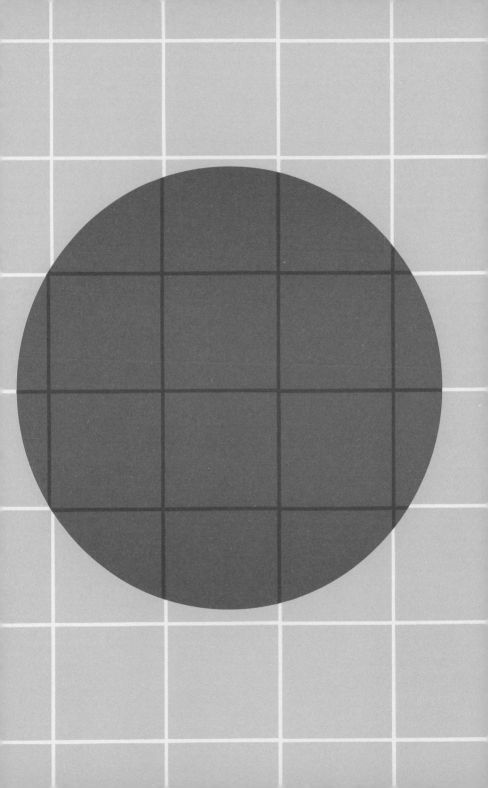

What's Motivating You?

Your motivation to create something likely comes from a very personal place, as if you're holding something inside you and need to find a way to externalize it. Are there external factors (i.e., recognition, compensation, accolades) that motivate you? Take a moment to jot down all of the reasons why you make what you make.

_____

_____

_____

_____

_____

_____

_____

_____

_____

_____

_____

_____

_____

_____

_____

_____

_____

_____

"I am a goal-oriented person. I love giving myself requirements in my practice. I think that's how I started making art. I told myself that I would make a zine every month. That led to me going to the studio early mornings before my shift at my service job and forcing myself to finish something."

Emma Kohlmann
(Visual artist)

What's Your Goal?

A goal is a clearly defined objective, a finished product
that you are striving to bring into the world. List some
creative projects that you're pursuing or would like to
pursue. Which of these projects feels like the most important
one to you? Circle it—we'll keep coming back to this one.

—   —

—   —

—   —

—   —

—   —

—   —

—   —

—   —

—   —

Intentions and Goals

Set Your Intention

If you can describe the intrinsic reward for making something,
then you'll always be clear about the underlying intention of
your work. The end result might be disappointing, but you'll
know why you wanted to pursue the project in the first place.

Josh Fadem reads a list before going out onstage to perform
his comedy. Notice that it's entirely possible for him to
meet the intentions stated here, even if his set bombs. Try
drafting something similar for the creative project that you
circled on page 95.

_____

_____

_____

_____

_____

_____

_____

_____

_____

_____

_____

_____

"address something
keep going
if you're shouting to no
response, get quiet
show must go on
be comfortable onstage
don't rely on anything
enjoy failing
nerves are just unknown
address the big picture
stretch
do the splits
start from where you're at
emotionally."

Josh Fadem
(Actor/comedian, *30 Rock*,
Better Call Saul, *Twin Peaks*)

Motivated by the Process

"I like to locate a really ludicrous, far-flung aspect of the project and play with it in writing or thinking till a very unlikely door opens to reenter the main project through."

Eileen Myles
(Poet/writer, author of *Chelsea Girls*)

The creative process is rarely cut-and-dried. We can analyze it and try breaking it down into steps and sections and flowcharts, but it's a messy and unpredictable journey that is often hard to replicate. There's a cliché that the journey matters more than the destination, and many artists do rely on their process to shape the final product, rather than being motivated by a clear endgame.

Prem Krishnamurthy, who works as a designer as well as a curator and teacher, says this about his approach: "I usually have persistent medium- to longer-term goals, which emerge periodically. But I usually forget about them and instead try to focus on small, incremental steps. Whenever I look back at my old notebooks, I notice that I'm slowly making progress on these larger goals. Yet I find that staring at the end goals can be a bit depressing and also alienates me from the creative process, as opposed to taking it week by week, day by day, which is more productive."

It's perfectly valid to state your goal, put it out of sight, and let the process take over so that you are open to new possibilities. Another strategy is to have a main idea in mind, but to find an indirect route to explore it (like Eileen Myles), because for you the process is the whole point.

Motivated by the Product

"I just become obsessed in my head with the finished painting, knowing it will be the best painting I have completed. It often is not, but if I didn't have that belief I would never finish a piece. I always hang a newly completed piece so that I see it fresh every day when I come into the studio. Sometimes there will be a passage in the work that I know could be better, but I will try and avoid reworking it right away—in the end it will be the only passage that jumps out at me, and that will make me go back in the next day."

Clive Smith
(Visual artist)

On the other hand, there's nothing wrong with holding on to something in your mind's eye that you desperately want to create. There are plenty of artists who are motivated by achieving a final product and view their process as a series of steps to getting there. There can still be learning along the way, of course, but the process doesn't determine or drastically reshape the end result.

If you relate to this type of creativity, try Clive Smith's approach. How might it apply to your medium or discipline? If you leave a thread unstitched or a sentence unedited, does it bring you back to your project?

Product or Process?

Do you draw motivation from your destination: the vision of what you want to create? Or do you prefer a more process-oriented approach, in which you won't know what the final product is going to be until you are well along the journey? There is no wrong answer, and you may identify with a bit of both.

_____

_____

_____

_____

_____

_____

_____

_____

_____

_____

_____

_____

_____

_____

_____

_____

_____

Quotas and Deadlines

You have a creative goal and you've set aside the time to work toward it. How do you gauge whether the time spent has been "productive"? What will give you the feeling of a job well done when you wrap up for the day? If you are accustomed to working in an environment where deadlines, standards, and deliverables are clear, you're likely to get frustrated when you try to map those expectations onto your creative pursuits. Or maybe not. As always, there are different ways of looking at this:

"I'm very anti-productivity, or rather, anti the tyranny of productivity in purely late-capitalist terms. I'm repulsed by the notion that our moral or social worth is indexed to our output. When it comes to writing, I don't think there's much correlation between efficiency (a cognate of productivity) and merit. As in, my first novel took me about six years [to write], I wrote the bulk of my second novel in two months: It definitely doesn't mean the latter is better, or vice versa.

Hermione Hoby
(Writer, critic, author of *Neon in Daylight*)

"It's a capitalist assembly line. Henry Ford. The Amazon fulfillment center. Number goals. And like Amazon, I usually set impossible goals for myself. I'm always behind. The 'boss' is always pissed at me and I'm always stressed about not meeting my numbers. Shit, I'm ten paintings behind. Shit, now I'm twenty paintings behind. But that's pushing me. Maybe it's masochistic, but it works."

Cynthia Daignault*
(Visual artist, writer, musician)

*Stosuy, Brandon, "Cynthia Daignault on Not Commodifying Your Art," Creative Independent, October 7, 2016.

Creative Accounting

Think about your own relationship to the opposing views on the previous pages. Do quotas and deadlines help push your creative process, or do you find them to be unnecessary and limiting?

_____

_____

_____

_____

_____

_____

_____

_____

_____

_____

_____

_____

_____

_____

_____

_____

Can you think of a way to apply the opposite approach to your current process? What might happen if you set some productivity expectations for yourself—or freed yourself from them?

_____

_____

_____

_____

_____

_____

_____

_____

_____

_____

_____

_____

_____

_____

_____

_____

_____

_____

_____

Map One Goal

Choose a creative goal from your list on page 95 and try mapping out the steps for completing it in a flowchart. If it will help, assign deadlines for the key steps in your process.

The Blindfold

Chelsea Hodson mentioned to me once that she sometimes writes while blindfolded. I thought this was an interesting strategy, so I asked her to explain it a bit more. It turns out that the blindfold helps her get the necessary distance from herself (and her own self-criticism) to push into new creative territory:

> "In writing some of my essays, I became so horrified by what I was revealing that I simply couldn't look at it. For me, there is a push and pull to writing—the desire to lean into my obsessions, but also the instinct to run away from them. I found that by blindfolding myself, I could remain present while writing things that I wasn't yet ready to face. I never sit down to write like, 'Yeah, this is fun!' It's what I want to do, but, at the same time, I have to trick myself into saying what I really mean."

I'm struck by the idea of using a blindfold to remove yourself from the creative process when you're getting in your own way. Having a vision for your work and setting ambitious goals sounds great, but not if the weight of your expectations keeps you from exploring, pushing beyond your comfort zone, or even beginning at all. It's interesting to think about what you could learn if you danced, painted, sewed, or played your instrument blindfolded.

Maybe the results would be revelatory, or even brilliant. If not, you can always just blame it on the blindfold.

Reflections

Experiment with doing your work blindfolded, or with some kind
of constraint that limits your control and removes the pressure
to perform. Describe this experience and the results:

_____

_____

_____

_____

_____

_____

_____

_____

_____

_____

_____

_____

_____

_____

_____

_____

_____

_____

_____

Creative Juggling

> "I let a simple idea or rule play out and see what kind of thing begins to manifest. I let it tell me what it wants to be. So, because I work this way, having other pots on the stove, simmering, works well— each thing gets moved along incrementally. That requires a fairly organized mind-set, allocating time and schedule, which I know can be difficult for some folks, though I think it's a skill set one can easily develop and master."

David Byrne
(Multimedia creator,
front person of Talking Heads)

In my personal work, I like to juggle a few things at once, and often don't fully realize what I'm doing or where the real opportunity rests until I'm already deep into the process. Many of the things I've done have been invented and cobbled together ad hoc as I go along. I think that's fine—it's a way of working that's kept me open to possibility and helped me avoid missing potential opportunities.

Although I like to remain receptive and flexible when it comes to the bigger picture, I show up daily for my creative projects. I focus on a "slow and steady" approach and write for an hour or two a day. I don't fixate on how much I write during that period. I put in the time and don't worry too much about the results, because I'll be there again tomorrow.

This sort of simmering has worked well for me because, practically speaking, there is only so much time I can spend on a specific project before burning out, and moving between things keeps me fresh. If I stick to one thing for too long, that's when I start checking social media or reading the news, or otherwise lose focus.

I lift weights with my friend John Sharian, who works as an actor. One day he pointed out that if you stop between repetitions, it's harder to get going again because you're beginning from a dead spot. He suggested creating a rhythm. I've thought of how this relates to my creative work: I do a lot of projects at once so I can move between things with fewer stops.

Exercise offers a good metaphor for creativity. You get inspired one day and go for a run. The next day you shock yourself by shaking off the hesitation and getting off the couch again. Then you keep doing it, eventually without even thinking about it. You no longer need to psych yourself up; it just happens. You made it happen, and then you keep making it happen.

On Finishing

> "When something's done, I'll go, 'OK, cool,' and I'll shelve it, and I'll rejoice that the damn thing is done and my desktop is empty so I can fill it with the next project. I'm a shipbuilder. I don't want to sail in them. I want you to sail in them. I'm just happy that they leave the harbor so I can have an empty workspace."
>
> Henry Rollins*
> (Singer-songwriter, musician, writer, actor)

Once, when I spoke to the punk icon Henry Rollins, he explained that he builds things because he needs the process of creation in his life, and once a project is done, he lets it sail away without further thought. At that point, people can interact with his projects in any way they want to—they can sail in them or shoot them down—and he's on to the next thing.

Not everyone has that kind of mind-set. Sometimes there's fear in completing a project. Have you experienced this? The journey feels safe, and even pleasurable, but once it's done, it goes out into the world and then what? What if it's no good? For instance, think about what model, artist, and musician Brooks Ginnan says about finishing and releasing a creative project:

"The journey of creation is my favorite—and the most fulfilling—part. Yet, I find it difficult many days. While the feeling of completing something and letting go is nearly unrivaled in my head, I can't help but feel afraid of the what-

*Stosuy, Brandon, "Henry Rollins on Defining Success," Creative Independent, March 27, 2017.

ifs that accompany the end result. 'How will it be received?' 'Will anyone actually care?' 'Does this make a difference for anyone but me?' All the usual bits of imposter syndrome, I suppose. But if making it truly is the best part, why should it even matter what anyone thinks?"

Letting Go

Do you think of yourself as a shipbuilder who can easily let a project sail off into the sunset? Do you enjoy sharing the finished product? Or do you find it hard to wrap something up and share it (because it could always be different or better)?

Conclusion

"There's love in not knowing what else you're good at and clinging to the thing you are good at with everything you've got. The journey is all I have. I'm not always happy with the end result, and my anxiety disorders don't always let me enjoy the way the product moves through the world. But I am good at the journey. I'm at my most honest when I have to answer to myself about what is and isn't working, even before anyone else sees it."

Hanif Abdurraqib

(Poet/writer, author of *They Can't Kill Us Until They Kill Us*, *A Fortune for Your Disaster*, and *Go Ahead in the Rain*)

The purpose of this section is to explore what drives you to create and whether you tend to be process-driven or goal-driven in your creative pursuits. Your approach likely shifts between these modes depending on the phase of your project. It's useful to keep asking yourself which mind-set will help you stay invested in the work. Right now, do you need a timeline and marks to hit, or do you need to meander and let go of expectations?

Goals often shift because you usually need more than one day to work on a project. New goals are set as your process unfolds. Over time, your underlying intentions may shift, too. The reason why you are making something—what you hope to get out of the experience—is an ongoing question to engage in your practice. If you are clear on this, then any amount of time spent on a creative project will feel worthwhile, and worth returning to again and again.

The thing that needs to be consistent is your ability to keep going. Different artists have different ways of making this happen. Here, I've emphasized a few things that work for me and many of the artists that I've spoken to about their creative process. Much of it boils down to creating routines and habits that allow you to show up for your work and make incremental progress. But if you are having difficulty connecting the incremental work to the bigger picture (why am I doing this?) and are feeling unmotivated as a result, then stop and consider these questions:

> What is the intrinsic reward for doing what you are doing?

> How would you feel about your work if nobody else ever saw it or experienced it?

> Is your current project meeting your intentions, even if you aren't meeting your goals?

> Is it time to reassess your creative goals?

> Are you letting your goals get in the way of the process?

> How quickly after achieving a goal do you set new ones?

"I haven't found a real balance yet. I've just figured out how to keep my body and mind from fully breaking down, and the creative productivity can come or not come— but I don't have the capacity to worry about that."

Mitski*

(Singer-songwriter, *Puberty 2, Be the Cowboy*)

*Stosuy, Brandon, "Question: How Do You Balance Health and Productivity?" Creative Independent, 2018.

In the previous chapter, we looked at the difference between goals and intention and discussed the way an intention is something internal and present throughout your process (your journey) and a goal is something external to you that you hope to achieve (your destination).

Throughout this book, I've emphasized the importance of working on your creative projects habitually and embracing the incremental progress that you can make with any amount of time that you can find for your work.

However, most of the artists that I've spoken to have questioned the idea that creativity can be optimized. And certainly, it's not humanly possible to be productive all the time. But perhaps that depends on how you define productivity. If stepping back from your work means that you come back to it rested, with new ideas or a shift in perspective, then wouldn't you consider downtime to be productive?

This chapter is about making sure to schedule downtime into your creative process. It's useful learning to feel yourself moving toward potential burnout, and knowing when to fit breaks into your day to day. When we get caught up in deadlines and to-do lists, we lose sight of the essential fact that we are more than what we produce.

I was talking to Jia Tolentino, who had just recently published *Trick Mirror*, a book of essays. She explained that when she takes a break, she really takes a break: She shuts off the work part of her brain, turns off her phone for two days, sets aside time to walk her dog in the park, and meets with friends. She does this intentionally. It's time to recuperate. It's a positive use of downtime, and it allows her to return to her work with renewed energy.

A singer who belts out at their greatest volume with no dynamic variation grows grating. People who work out too much wear down their bodies. This is true for the creative life, too: Even if you're "in the zone" and creating consistently, you shouldn't be afraid to pause. It makes for a stronger dynamic. You need to allow yourself to do things that don't necessarily scan as "productive."

It's hard to believe we need to force ourselves to take breaks. Time is scarce, and it can be scary to spend time on something that seems unproductive. Honestly, I can have trouble disconnecting this way. I get caught up in the idea of forward momentum and worry that if I stop, I'll have a harder time starting up again.

But not working really can help your work—whether that means your creative work or your job. You've chosen to create something because it gives you a sense of identity beyond your paid work and other responsibilities. The flip side is that you also need to reaffirm your value outside of your creative work. I was cleaning out a drawer and found a note my mother had written to me shortly before I went off to college. In it she said,

"Remember to pace yourself and enjoy life . . . you cannot do it all in 'one day.'"

I like that she put "one day" in quotes. It seems to suggest that "one day" could be different depending on what it is you're working on or trying to complete. "One day" for a novelist might be different than "one day" for a poet or a chef or a gardener. She was right: You don't need to complete everything in a day. Things take time, and it's OK to give your project the time it needs.

In the note, she also reminded me to "be kind to yourself." This is important. If you want to keep moving, you need to be kind to yourself, respect yourself, and respect the process itself.

"My day job genuinely fulfills my creative instincts and provides me with pleasure. That being said, I'm on guard against becoming accustomed to searching for so much personal fulfillment in work. The fact that work is fun for me means that I haven't done anything in a long time that was purely for fun, purely for experimentation. My book felt a lot like that (if not totally like that) for a while, which was amazing. Then it came out, and actually promoting it was the thing that made me recategorize the book as work."

Jia Tolentino
(*The New Yorker* staff writer, author of *Trick Mirror*)

When Art Become Work

Can you identify any moments in your creative endeavors where the lifting gets heavy, and what started out as a hobby or a passion project now feels like work? Describe some examples of how work and play are blurred in your life:

_____

_____

_____

_____

_____

_____

_____

_____

_____

_____

_____

_____

_____

_____

_____

_____

_____

_____

_____

"I have no rules or a plan to follow as an artist, so doing activities that have instructions or a clear start and finish help me to keep a healthy mind-set. Cooking and baking, or following a recipe someone else has worked out, is incredibly satisfying."

Clive Smith
(Visual artist)

"Turning off my phone. Leaving the house. Looking at paintings. Laughing uncontrollably. Crying in a theater. Cuddling with my cat. Dancing until my body can't anymore. Being more present in the physical world. Being less present in the digital world."

Brooks Ginnan
(Performance artist, musician, model)

"I suppose the only things that qualify as truly not work are the wholly mindless things, or rather, the things that occupy my mind with pleasant blankness. That would include cooking: I enter a distinctive state of humming stupidity while I cook."

Hermione Hoby
(Writer, critic, author of *Neon in Daylight*)

"I started a choir. I have no business running a choir as I don't sing well at all, but it's a beautiful way to get into my body."

Tina Roth Eisenberg
(Founder of *swissmiss*, Tattly, and CreativeMornings)

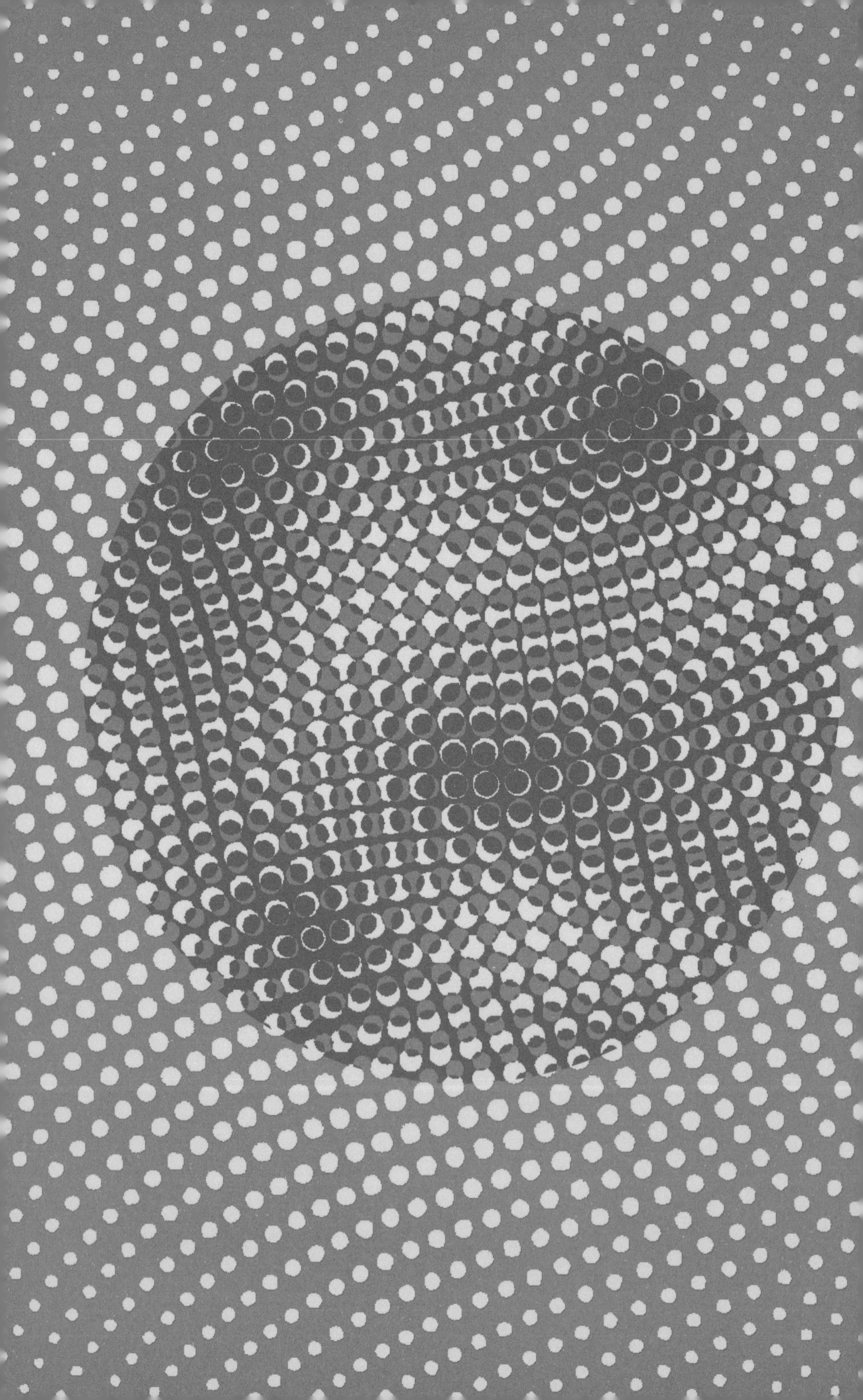

"So many of my longtime close friends aren't writers and aren't particularly invested in the world of writing. And they knew me well before I wrote anything. Not even anything worthwhile, just anything. I think I am at my most healthy when I have a reminder that to some people, I'm more than what I produce."

Hanif Abdurraqib
(Poet/writer, author of
They Can't Kill Us Until They Kill Us,
A Fortune for Your Disaster, and
Go Ahead in the Rain)

Time Out

Take a moment to describe any activities that are truly
relaxing for you. Do you turn to something that uses a
different mental process then the rest of your work (like
Clive Smith, who can relax when he has directions to follow)?
Is there anything that you enjoy doing without any pressure
to be good at it (like Tina Roth Eisenberg's feelings about
being in a choir)?

_____

_____

_____

_____

_____

_____

_____

_____

_____

_____

_____

_____

_____

_____

Redefine "Busy"

"When making any kind of daily task list I'll regularly include tasks for my health. It makes me pause when I'm working to think, 'OK, I wanted to stretch today, take a moment to do that.' This gives me a simple reminder and then I can cross a health-related task off my list with the other various endeavors, which feels very satisfying."

Lavender Suarez
(Musician, sound healer who performs as C. Lavender)

What if we try to redefine what it means to be "busy"? What if being busy involved resting, taking care of ourselves, and working on our relationships with other human beings? We can get fixated on our to-do lists, so it's important to be mindful of what goes on them and how we can shift this tool from being burdensome to helpful.

We tend to only add appointments and meetings to our calendars. Try adding things like "take a walk," "grab some coffee," and "daydream" to your schedule. When these appointments pop up in your calendar, treat them like you would any other obligation. Jenny Hval has adopted this practice: "I think I need to put in rituals in my calendar so I can deal with looking at it so much, and to give myself space to do nothing, too. Because that's the time in which everything happens."

Prem Krishnamurthy has a specific way of refreshing throughout the day: "In late 2018, I started to practice my own form of meditation that I call 'Counting.' It uses both hands and the voice in synch to count to very high numbers. I might count to 1080 or higher in a given day—which means about twenty to thirty minutes of meditation. This is a useful one for me, as it keeps me off of my phone or computer and forces me to focus. Before that, I used to take power naps periodically during the day to reset my brain, but now the meditation tends to do a similar thing."

Press Pause

It's important to pause, especially on a hectic day. It may feel like you're detaching your mind—and you are—but you'll realize as you incorporate these kinds of things into your practice that nothing is mindless or useless. Write down some things that you can do to change focus or take breaks.

When I have five minutes, I can:

_____

_____

_____

When I have fifteen minutes, I can:

_____

_____

_____

When I have thirty minutes, I can:

_____

_____

_____

_____

Walking With No Time

Try taking a walk with no time, as Sigrid Lauren describes it on the facing page. When you get back, write your impressions (what you noticed, how you felt) here:

_____

_____

_____

_____

_____

_____

_____

_____

_____

_____

_____

_____

_____

_____

_____

_____

_____

_____

"Walking with no time means deciding to go for a walk with no destination in mind. It involves noticing the subtleties along the way and choosing to enjoy them. I make a choice to notice the things I would usually not, like seeing a strange bush and touching it, admiring it, sitting beside it for a minute, and being open to impulses and the beauty I otherwise pass by when I need to be somewhere at a certain time. During these walks, I will listen to music or a podcast, but I make sure to turn it off at some point and really listen to the environment around me."

Sigrid Lauren
(Dancer, choreographer, performance artist, member of FlucT)

What Is "Productive"?

It is easy to get caught up in being "productive" in a way that isn't healthy, or that actually gets in the way of creativity. Justin Vernon* of Bon Iver once remarked to me: "I'll always love the project. But I definitely have to leave it from time to time, otherwise it's just too much focus and too much energy surrounding an idea that it is just a band, just a project idea. It's not more than that." Think about the ways that Hanif Abdurraqib and Hermione Hoby view productivity.

"The truth is, I'm several other things before I'm a writer. I'm a friend, a partner, a dog owner, a sports fan, a bad movie lover, a music nerd. I have to check all of those boxes before I can even consider myself a good writer, or someone who can write well. I can't write well if I'm not serving the other parts of my life that need to be served. And I believe that serving those parts of my life can also be a type of production. Production, for me at this stage in my life, is anything that makes a return to the page easier."

Hanif Abdurraqib
(Poet/writer, author of *They Can't Kill Us Until They Kill Us*, *A Fortune for Your Disaster*, and *Go Ahead in the Rain*)

*Stosuy, Brandon, "On the Power of Cooperation," Creative Independent, June 21, 2018.

"Of course it feels great to end a day having written four thousand words (happens rarely), but it also feels great to have spent a day living honestly, whatever that might mean for that particular day. Counseling a friend in need for five hours is 'productive': It produces solace for them, it produces a deepening of friendship for us, and it produces some small good in the world. If I'm sick, a day spent in bed is 'productive.' It is producing my health. Similarly, doing nothing but reading a very good novel all day is 'productive.' I have nothing to show for it, but I know that I'm enriched, I'll feel the peace of a day well spent."

Hermione Hoby
(Writer, critic, author of *Neon in Daylight*)

Pieces of You

Fill the circles on these pages with words and descriptions
representing pieces of your identity that have seemingly
nothing to do with your work or creative projects (similar to
what Hanif Abdurraqib does on the previous page).

Is a piece of you being neglected? Draw a ring around this circle; we'll come back to it.

Field Trip

Each year I take a break when my wife and kids and I go on vacation in northern interior Maine. We visit the cabin that my wife's grandmother bought in the sixties. It's in a tiny town (population: eighty) that never changes. It also doesn't get cell reception. As I mentioned before, I work off of momentum and worry about losing it. But when I'm forced to disengage in this way, things happen.

While in Maine a few summers ago, I first got the general seed in mind for a project that ultimately led, a couple years later, to this book. It didn't take long. I sat down to watch the sunset, was inspired by how slow things were moving, and thought about creating a kind of "how to" that focused not on building things, but on building the creative process itself (a blueprint of sorts).

In *The Artist's Way*, a self-help book written in 1992 by Julia Cameron, the reader is instructed to take weekly field trips. The field trips are meant to be time spent alone, treating yourself to an intentional act of inspiration. You might go to a park or a museum, or a restaurant a few neighborhoods over.

A vacation may not be practical for you right now, but you can probably plan a field trip. Flip back to pages 136–137, where you listed different dimensions of yourself and circled one that has been neglected. Where would you go and what would you do if you put that part of yourself in charge?

Report Back

Take a field trip; jot down where you went, why you chose
that spot, and any important takeaways about that day.

_____

_____

_____

_____

_____

_____

_____

_____

_____

_____

_____

_____

_____

_____

_____

_____

_____

_____

Hitting a Wall

"I am not the type of person who can sit down every day and make something new. I'm absolutely a type B personality with an inability to make something in a linear way, but I think the days that I try to and find myself coming up short and hitting a wall, I know it is better to stop than to continue. This is surely not something I've always accepted as valid, but in time, it's become a far healthier method of creation than beating a dead horse and subsequently hating myself."

Brooks Ginnan
(Performance artist, musician, model)

Not all breaks happen by choice. Sometimes, you get blocked. You grab your coffee, you sit down with your laptop or get out your tools or supplies, and nothing happens. You set aside a couple of hours to work on the thing you normally love to work on and you just can't get in the mood to work on it. Does this mean it's no longer your passion project? Are you no longer a gardener, a painter, a chef, a dancer?

No project comes together perfectly without hiccups. If someone ever told you otherwise, they were lying. Creative blocks, creative anxiety, perfectionism, and distraction in its many forms (from social media to that nagging voice in your head) are all common and natural. I like to think of these so-called blocks as creative downtime. The most important thing in these situations is to go with the flow, to set a time when you will come back to the project, and to reassure yourself that this roadblock doesn't mean you've reached a dead end.

Conclusion

"In a lovely way, it's all work. That's what it is to be a writer. I'm writing all the time, even if it's only mentally, because language is where I live. I can't live anywhere else, and everything I live is material, even if only in an oblique way. The weird image or gratifyingly fully formed sentence that comes into my head while hiking is work. Literal dreaming is 'work' when I wake up with a shred of something that turns into a scene or a plot fix."

Hermione Hoby

(Writer, critic, author of *Neon in Daylight*)

What if you think of everything—including creative blocks and downtime—as part of your overall project? Mike Hadreas, who records music under the name Perfume Genius, has told me that even when he isn't working, he has ideas cycling through the back of his brain, so when he does sit down to work, he feels like he's already been moving toward something new.

This chapter was about making sure to schedule downtime into your creative process. It can be easy to burn out, and recovery time is important. When we get caught up in deadlines and to-do lists, we also get caught up in not stopping, and then our creative projects start taking on the undesirable aspects of work (i.e., obligation, isolating toil, and overly rigid definitions of results).

As much as it's useful to move away from the idea of productivity for productivity's sake, you do want to complete things, even if it takes a while. It's easier to do this when you know what you need to stay in the right place both physically and mentally. Simply put: What are some practices that help you maintain a healthy mind-set?

You've spent some time defining these practices in this chapter, but this kind of self-observation is ongoing. Keep asking yourself:

> What are some things that you do that definitely are not work? What does relaxing look like to you? What does play mean to you?

> When you get busy, what aspects of yourself are you most likely to neglect?

> Even when you're busy, what aspects of wellness are the easiest for you to maintain?

> How do you shake off an unproductive day? Can you reframe productivity so that it embraces more of who you are, rather than simply what you produce?

> When you are overwhelmed and stressed, have you tried shifting your mind-set by taking field trips and aimless walks?

Further Thoughts

Acknowledgments

Since I began pasting zines together as a teenager, everything I've worked on creatively has, in some way or another, gone into this book. Each thing we do is part of a continuum, so please consider this list of thank-yous ongoing.

There are, for starters, the folks whose names are in it. They answered my questions about how they do what they do with honesty and intelligence, and I appreciate it. Their words are essential—without them, this is all much less interesting.

I also want to thank my editor, Karrie Witkin, who felt more like a collaborator than an editor, and whose insights and creativity (and endurance!) shaped so much of what you see here.

Then there are the people whose names are not already listed somewhere in *Make Time for Creativity*, but without whom the book wouldn't exist. For instance, my agent Chad Luibl—patient, insightful, intelligent, a legit death-metal drummer—has been an untiring advocate. And, of course, my family, who show up here and there in the anecdotes I wrote, but even when not mentioned, are a part of everything else I do: I love you Jane, Henry, and Jake.

Finally, thanks to the people who've already answered my questions for Volume 2, and who you'll be hearing from next time.